To: Zillah
May God continue
To bless you!
~Rev Kim

RESTORED

By Kimberly Walker

Restored

ISBN: 978-1-938950-74-2

Greater is He Publishing
9824 E. Washington St,
Chagrin Falls Ohio 44023
P O. Box 39283 Solon Ohio, 44139

Dedication

Dedicated to
My Mother, Delores Walker
&
My Son, Bryan B. Walker
Rest in Heaven
Special Thanks to My Children,
Ryan, Clairissa, & Julian (son-in-law)
Thank you so much for keeping me encouraged. Your love and support speaks volumes.
My Dad, Bronic Walker Sr.,
Thank you for loving me enough to let go and allow God.
My Best Friend, Debra Mueller,
Thank you for going on every adventure and being one of my biggest cheerleaders! Your friendship is irreplaceable.
My Spiritual Mom, Dr. Victoria F. Dorsey,
Thank you for seeing the best in me when I couldn't see it in myself.
My Church Family of Fifth Church of God
"City of Deliverance"

Contents

Chapter 1 - How It Started (Baby Steps)

Two years ago from today, I, being a union carpenter and church member, was given the great task to build a wooden cross for the Easter program. To many, this might seem like child's play. After all, how hard is it to make a cross? Just take two pieces of wood and nail them together perpendicular to each other. While this may be the general idea, I knew the importance of building the cross because it held significant purpose, as it was symbolic of God's love and the joy of my salvation.

That week, I was on the lookout for the materials needed to create the cross. I knew I needed rope, nails, sandpaper, etc., but I was especially looking for the wood. It didn't matter what type of wood it was, as in oak or cedar, but I was more concerned about the character of the wood.

One day as I was leaving a job site, I noticed a pile of coiled steel laying on top of some wood. As I got closer,

I got excited because I knew I'd finally found the wood I was looking for. After loading the abandoned wood into my vehicle, I couldn't help but wonder why would anyone throw such beautiful wood away. When I got home, I found the answer to my question. The wood had some blemishes and other flaws that most people would look at as imperfect, which was probably why it was discarded and left at the bottom of a junk pile. Some people did not share my sentiment, telling me I was doing too much and advised me to replace it with new wood. I guess that's what makes me different; while most people would simply replace, I chose to restore. I will finish the story of this wood later, but first let me share a little background about myself.

I grew up in Garfield Heights, a small suburb outside of Cleveland, Ohio. Growing up, I've always felt like I didn't fit in with the many other boys and girls in my neighborhood. I guess it was because, in reality, my problems were much different than theirs. While they were worried about things kids tend to worry about, such as getting the latest toy or being able to spend the night at each other's houses, I was worried about who was going to violate me sexually. This may seem like the beginning of a tragic story, but the real tragedy is that it happens more often than you would think. These types of crimes are usually carried out by someone close to the family or within the family. David Finkelhor, Director of the Crimes Against Children Research Center (CACRC), reported in The National Center for Victims of Crime (NCVC) website that:

- 1 in 5 girls and 1 in 20 boys is a victim of child sexual abuse;
- Self-report studies show that 20% of adult females and 5-10% of adult males recall a childhood sexual assault or sexual abuse incident;
- During a one-year period in the U.S., 16% of youth ages 14 to 17 had been sexually victimized;
- Over the course of their lifetime, 28% of U.S. youth ages 14 to 17 had been sexually victimized;
- Children are most vulnerable to CSA between the ages of 7 and 13.

Sadly, by the age of 3, I had already fallen prey to each statistic above. I carried that sick secret the babysitter introduced me to for a while. I was afraid to say anything to anyone who could have helped me. Today, I know that the true weapon used in these types of assault isn't pornography, fondling, or penetration. In fact, it's not of a sexual nature at all. Secrecy and fear are the true weapons. It dates way back to the beginning of man. When sin first reared its evil head in the Garden of Eden, it was followed by secrecy and fear. Grace and mercy go together like secrecy and fear because where you will find one you will usually find the other. It took God's grace and a lot of mercy to pull me away from the secrecy and fear which had interrupted my young, innocent life.

Now that you know the nature and content of this book, there is something I would like to address before I go any further into the text. While this book is filled with accounts of sorrow, pain, neglect, abuse, and more, all seemingly directed towards a helpless young child, this book isn't for those who seek revenge upon their attacker(s) for subjecting them to similar scenarios as described in my stories. This book was written out of strength, not weakness; courage, not fear; love, not hate. I've learned that sometimes the greatest decisions of your life are made at the lowest positions of your life. I've also learned that God has ways of turning things around. The story of Joseph is proof that you can go to the lowest of lows and still be selected and anointed to do something great.

Job would tell you that greatness isn't weighed by what's been taken from you, but by what you give back. In spite of what's been done or taken from us, God still deserves our praise. With that being said, opaque and covered hearts will not be able to receive this message. This book was written in truth and transparency, therefore in truth and transparency must it be received. My goal of this book is to spark a fire. That fire is your testimony; it proclaims to the enemy that you're restored and rekindled. I want people who have been in similar situations to speak up and speak out by sharing their testimonies with others who are still as lost, afraid, and broken as I was. There are people who will open up if you share your story. I, being part of the clergy, encourage and challenge other clergymen and women to open up about their stories so that lives will be changed. This book is intended to give hope to the hopeless.

Let's take a breather from that chapter of my life

and talk about someone I truly love: my grandmother. She was truly a gentle and strong woman of God. I never once heard her raise her voice. (I can't speak for anyone else.) She was a beautiful woman and carried herself as such. I can still remember the sweet smell of peach cobbler pie seeping from her small oven, which sat neatly in her kitchen.

"You been a good girl?" she would ask me, and I would shy away because even then at the young age of six, I already had major issues and low self-esteem. I guess I couldn't answer her question wholeheartedly because I felt like a bad girl due to the abuse and trickery of my abusers. My mind had been conditioned to believe that it was my fault and that people would look at me differently if I told them what was going on; this included my beloved grandmother.

Of course, that was just a lie my abuser used to prevent me from talking. Lying is another weapon of the enemy that works hand in hand with secrecy and fear. "Lying covers the secrecy, and fear causes you to lie." It's a vicious cycle that can only be broken by the truth. In the garden of Eden, lies from the serpent led to Adam and Eve covering up their nakedness with fig leaves (secrecy) in fear of God. This type of pressure should never enter the mind of a six-year-old. However, there I was, constantly covering up one lie for another. My grandmother had a way of making me feel normal. I remember how she would get us around her chair, open up her Bible, and tell us about a man named Jesus and how he loves us no matter what. I couldn't believe there was such a person in this world who would love me unconditionally! Those words caught my attention because I had started to only believe in conditional love. It seemed like I had to do what I didn't want to do in order for others to be okay with me. Now, I heard Grandma talking about this wonderful man named Jesus who wanted to be my friend! It was at this point that I said, "Grandma, I want to know him. I want him to be my friend."

When you are six years old, the word "friend" is associated with fun, and your level of trust is contingent upon how much fun your friend provides. But when you are older, the word "friend" is associated with trust, and that trust is contingent upon the amount of time spent with and knowledge of that friend. This is the basic principle of the popular phrase we teach our children known as "Stranger Danger." Because kids can be tricked with elementary tactics such as candy, fun, and toys. This makes them easy targets as they may look at those who offer them such things as friend. When the parent has a friend or family member that hurts the child, it makes the "Stranger Danger" approach difficult to recognize immediately. It can confuse a kid, or even a teenager, about what's normal and abnormal behavior when it concerns family or friends of the family.

A friend of mine was telling me about a time when he was at a circus watching elephants do all sorts of tricks, from standing on balls to rolling over. He couldn't help but wonder how the small, skinny elephant trainer got such a big creature to follow his instruction. What is the purpose of placing such a small rope on such a great animal, knowing he could easily break that rope in half?

Months had passed, but finally, he received the answer to his question as he was watching a TV show that explained the process of capturing elephants. The poachers get in close to the elephants' camp and offer food while keeping their distance. Without warning, the poachers attack the male elephants and then the female elephants. At first, it looks like a slaughter, but after the male and female elephants are captured or killed, the poachers turn their attention to the young. That was the intended target. The young elephants are smaller and easier to intimidate and manipulate. Men place giant chains on the elephant and take him into captivity. They remove all the chains except the ones on his leg, and for a season, that baby elephant fights hard to break the chain. After a while, the baby elephant, who has grown a little in stature, stops struggling with the chain. In his mind, he can't break it. Not only that, because of the struggle, he has developed a sore on his leg and it hurts to move. The baby elephant begins to set borders for himself and refuses to go past those borders, as he doesn't want to hurt his leg. The baby elephant grows even more in stature and the chain is replaced with a rope because it matters not what is attached to him, whether it be a heavy chain or string. In his mind, he is too weak to break it.

After hearing this, I thought to myself that this is my story and the story of so many others who have been captured and chained with some type of sin, vice, or habit. It is a true example of the agenda the enemy has in store for us. The Bible says in John 10:10, "The thief comes no more than to steal, and to kill and to destroy."

In the elephant's case, they killed off the male elephant, which represents the strength of the home. Then they stole his nourishment by capturing his mother. Finally, by placing a heavy burden, like a chain, on the baby elephant, it wasn't long before his will to fight was destroyed. Sometimes we make mistakes and we place chains on ourselves, and other times, we are simply minding our own business, only to become victims of someone else's struggle.

Many of you may relate to this story and know what it's like to struggle with a vice that you were never intended to carry. You know what it's like to be hurt by the chain of affliction and addiction. To be hurt because you trusted the wrong individuals, and allowed them to get too close to you. Maybe you know what it's like to set borders. Maybe it affects your personal life by dating someone and soon after things start to get serious, you back off because you are reminded of the past hurt. If this is your case, then you are in captivity and it's time to break free.

My friend said it was silly to him to see the great elephant enslaved and limited to a rope. But this is no different from seeing great mechanics without a garage, or great minds without a degree or a class to share that knowledge. The enemy can place us in chains, but he can't replace the natural gift and power within us. Had the baby elephant grown up with a father, he would have seen the strength of his father and realized that the same power was in him. No rope would have been able to hold him. Had he witnessed the love of his mother, he would have realized that you never give up on your dream and never limit yourself.

But many people walk around with great power and never know it because, at some point in their life, someone placed a chain on them and everyone knows their true potential but them. In today's time, trust issues are at an all-time high and the term "friend" has been greatly exaggerated thanks to social media, which allows you to friend just about anyone. But the Bible tells me that "there is a friend that sticks closer than a brother." He is the same friend who my grandma told me about so many years ago. A true friend would not watch you suffer and struggle with anything. A true friend would push you past your limits and borders because a true friend would recognize your strength and potential and simply tell you to step forward and be free. After hearing about Jesus and the love he has for me, I decided to no longer be a slave to my abuser. I was ready to take my first step.

The wood had some blemishes and other flaws which most people would look at as imperfect which is probably why it was discarded and left at the bottom of a junk pile. Some people did not share my sentiment, telling me I was doing too much and advising me to replace it with new wood. I guess that's what makes me different; while most people would simply replace, I chose to restore.

Job 14:16 NIV - Surely then you will count my steps but not keep track of my sin.

Have you ever experienced sexual abuse as a child or adult? What steps, if any, did you take or are you taking to end the abuse?

1.)Have you ever felt like the chained elephant in any areas of your life? What did it take for you to gather the strength to face your fear?

____

____

____

____

____

____

____

2.)Have you ever placed trust in the wrong people and gotten hurt? Was your response to build up a wall or to continue to see the good in others?

____

____

____

____

____

____

____

3.)Do you remember how it felt when you were first introduced to Jesus? Who made the introduction and how did it make you feel to know you had unconditional love from someone you'd never met?

Chapter 2 - Nothing

Though most people won't admit it, it is easy for some parents with two or more children have a favorite child. This has never been the case for me concerning my kids, but it goes without saying that it does happen in some homes. Some examples of this could be showing more interest in one child than the other, or consistently giving more to one child than the other. Maybe your praises are focused more on the child who receives the most awards and accolades.

These are considered the "Red Zones" of parenthood, and if we're not careful, it can cause abnormal sibling rivalry and competitiveness. Favoritism can also cause sub-emotional distress such as low self-esteem, a sense of not being valued, isolation, and hatred. So it's important to be cognizant when dealing with children in this regard because while favoritism isn't love, love is sometimes interpreted through favoritism. In today's society, favoritism is found in many homes throughout America, and at the age of 12, I was about to find out that my home was no different.

I would like to tell you that I finally said enough was enough and told my parents of the sexual abuse. I would like to tell you that my family showed compassion and my mom held me close and told me it would be okay. I would like to tell you that my accuser was punished in some way and sorrowfully repented for his wrong doing. I would like to tell you that the abuse came to an end immediately and my chain was broken. But that wouldn't be the truth. The truth is, as much as I thought I was ready to take my first step from the abuse, I realized it would require more than sheer determination. It would also require more time. I was only 6, and at 6 years old the world is a much bigger place, and you find out quickly where you stand on the food chain.

My abuser wasn't your stereotypical slum bucket, grimy old man looking to get his jollies off. But he was young, smart and of a subtle nature which assisted him in feigning innocence. On top of this, he was a family member with a lot of family backing and influence. He had gained his grand title of "Golden Boy" by doing well in school, which eventually paved his way to appearing on television. My granddad was still head and chief of the family, and whatever he found pleasing, the rest of the family usually followed suit. In my granddad's eyes, my abuser could do no wrong as Granddad was blinded by his academic achievements and accolades. But I could see straight through him. I knew that, buried deep behind the awards and applause, was a dark secret of lust and lies. However, the support he received from the family was intimidating. How could I go to my mom or anyone and tell them what was going on without looking like the bad person?

I was truly in a mess, and to my knowledge, nothing like this had ever happened in my family. I would watch Superman and Wonder Woman cartoons and pretend that I was like them: a superhero. At the same time, I was constantly wondering who would come to my rescue? But there was nothing I could do besides try to cope with it all. I often thought that in some way, this was all my fault. Guilt is one of the heaviest things you can ever carry. I know this because I carried this guilt around with me and on me. My guilt came from thinking that bad things happen to bad people, so I would just pray to God that I would be a good girl.

I would hear my mom talk about other girls who were flirtatious with boys. She would call them "fast little girls." I didn't fully understand the entire definition, but I knew I didn't want to be in that category. So in school, I would sit at my desk with my hands folded, praying that God would make me a good girl. It had gotten so bad that it consumed my entire day and I couldn't focus on anything else because I just wanted to be a good girl. I felt that if I was a good girl, these bad things wouldn't happen to me anymore.

As a child, I thought that God was only at church, as if he was waiting for us to get there on Sunday. Grandma would continue to tell me about God, and I wanted to be close to God; however, I thought that in order to get closer to God, I had to go through the abuse. That's because my abuser lived at my grandparents' house and would abuse me every time I would visit. So if I wanted to go to Grandma's church, I had to go through that abuse. As I got older, I understood things better, but I still wanted to please God, and I felt like God was not pleased with me because of the hidden things that were going on.

My mom always said, "What's done in the dark will eventually come to light." I never knew I would actually witness it. It was a quiet summer day on Osborn Road. The birds were singing a new song as the fireflies and butterflies danced in the warm sweet air. I was their audience as I sat on the front porch in a mid-day daze. Abruptly, my mom came out and grabbed me by the arm, and we went to my grandparent's house.

I had no idea what was going on as my mom was quiet and had the deer-in-headlights look. Upon getting there, I remember wondering if I was in trouble but couldn't think as to why I would be. Finally, I was asked a string of questions leading to other strange questions concerning my abuser. My aunt caught my abuser red-handed in the act of sexually abusing both female and male family members who were younger than me. My heart stopped for a second.

"Did he do that to you as well?" I was asked.

I couldn't believe that after all this time, this nightmare was close to coming to an end! I also couldn't believe that I'd endured this torment and abuse for all of these years, and finally, my aunt breaks the case wide open. So when I was asked if this was done to me, I shamefully said, "YES!"

I grew up watching the court shows on TV, and I felt as if I was on a long episode of Matlock and we were finally nearing a verdict:

"Mr. Abuser, for your crimes of child endangerment and sexual abuse, how do you plead?"

And finally, the verdict:

"We, the jury, find you NOT GUILTY!"

Wait, what just happened? That's right, he received no punishment for what he did. Back then, it was somewhat taboo to air your dirty laundry around town, and it was decided by some of the family to keep our polished, award-winning student's name looking good. They decided to not let anyone know what really was going on. I was torn to pieces because I would dream of how good it would feel to finally tell someone and put an end to all of this.

I thought that I would feel heroic, but I felt horrible. I thought that I would feel healed, but I felt hurt. I thought that I would feel loved, but I felt lonely. Nothing was done. Everything was pretty much swept under the rug and me along with it. Nothing was done. I wasn't looking for his head on a stick, but how about a strict punishment of some sort? Nothing was done. I just wanted to feel protected. Nothing was done. I just wanted justice. Nothing was done! I just wanted assurance that these things can't happen without consequences. But nothing was done, and that day my name became nothing because I, too, was done.

From that day forward, I questioned my worth,

and I often would study other golden children and wonder, "How much wrong could they get away with?" I wondered, "Were they the prize trophy in their family?" I wondered, "Have they always lived a life of privilege?" I would ask myself, "What dark secrets are buried in their lives?" After studying the definition of the word "value," I learned that it means: the importance, worth, or usefulness of something.

Our society has a way of labeling people in conjunction with their social status. The rich and the poor are examples of this, yet these roles can be interchangeable as the rich can become the poor and the poor can become rich. The value of $100 is $100. It can never be less than its intended value even if it's cut in half. It has no depreciation. $100 yesterday is still $100 today. But what is the value of nothing? Nothing has no value. Zero, empty, loss, inefficient, broke, nobody, unknown etc. are all synonyms for nothing, and they all represent what I felt after nothing was done on my behalf. We, as a people, place price tags on the things we consider to be valuable. We look down on drug addicts, prostitutes, and the homeless to name a few, simply because of their social status.

I had been sexually abused since the age of 3 starting with the babysitter and leading to a family member and others after that. But as one chapter of my life was closing, another chapter was slowly falling apart. Every relationship has its troubles, but the relationship between my mom and dad was at a critical stage. The stage where counseling, time apart, or working it out was completely out of the question as they had reached the point of no return and the point of no reconciliation. Neither of them was innocent in the matter, but I have to give it to my dad for trying. He always tries to see the positive in every situation. He is the glass not half-empty, but half-full kind of guy. The kind of guy you would want in your corner for encouragement. My dad had proven this years earlier when he discovered that he was not the biological father of my little brother. Most men would have called it quits, but my dad stuck with it and not only accepted the fact, but he also gave my little brother his last name.

Through the years, the communication between my mom and dad became complicated. Eventually, my brother and I knew that things were at an all-time low when my parents started dragging us into their disputes. It was horrible: Dad would tell me or my brother to tell my mom something, and then my mom would tell me or my brother to tell my dad her response. This made my brother and me uncomfortable, and it only added to the issues.

Things got worse as time went by, and Dad was in and out of the house. We received few answers from my mom about what was going on. This pattern of here today gone tomorrow continued until one day, while my dad was preparing to leave, I remember grabbing him and begging him not to go. We sat on the porch and had a long talk in which he explained some things to me. I was only eleven years old and didn't understand it all, but one thing was for certain — I had to accept it. Life after that would never be the same, but my love for him never changed. I spent my summer breaks with him, and those were some of the best days of my life. It's no secret that I was, and still am, a daddy's girl, and, to this day, he is my true hero.

My mom was a real trooper for holding everything together in my father's absence. It's not my place to say who's to blame because it takes two to tango, and my parents had been doing the tango with each other for quite some time. But my mom was strong, and sometimes I think this is where I get my strength from. She was a nurse. Therefore, she was subjected to an unstable schedule. So when my dad left, she had to pick up longer, late night shifts. During that time, it was good and unusual for a young black woman, such as herself, to be able to do that. It taught us how to not make excuses for ourselves due to our circumstances.

However, sometimes good situations can also have bad consequences. My mom wanted out of her marriage and thought that she could do it all by herself. When she finally got what she asked for (figuratively speaking, not literally), she saw that it wouldn't be a simple walk in the park but a long, hard road that would soon take her attention away from her kids in order to focus on providing for them. I call this stage in life "Mud" because as a child, dating back from my abuse and through my deliverance, I learned that even when you pray for rain, you still have to deal with the mud. And my mom was about to deal with a lot of mud.

With my mom at work during the evenings, my house was the house to have a great party without the supervision of an adult, and all of my friends knew that. But do you remember when I told you about the mud that was internally building up? It wasn't inside of my house, but it was inside of me. You see, prior to being popular, I had carried the label "Nothing" in my head for so long. It identified me and minimized me. Now that I was known for something bad, it was better than not being known at all, so I counted it as good. If I could take a little time and talk to whoever is reading this book, especially young people, I would tell you to be careful of what you lay down with because you may not be able to quickly get up from it. The Bible says in Proverbs 27:20, "Hell and destruction are never full; so the eyes of man are never satisfied." These words would soon sum up a big portion of my young life.

"But nothing was done and that day my name became nothing, because I too, was done."

Romans 12:19 Do not take revenge, my dear friends, but leave room for God's wrath, for it is written: "It is mine to avenge; I will repay," says the Lord.

Have you or someone you know been a victim to injustice? How did it make you feel? What did you do to restore your self-value?

1.) Have you ever dreamt of a certain outcome during in a storm in your life and been totally disappointed with the outcome?

____

____

____

____

____

____

2.) Did you later discover the outcome was all a part of the larger plan God had for you?

____

____

____

____

____

____

3.) Have you ever felt devalued by the thoughts, words or actions of others? When did you come to the point of realization that your value is God-given?

4.) Have you ever looked for vindication in the wrong things (popularity, drugs, alcohol) only to find the solutions were only temporary? How did you come to terms with this?

5.) Have there been times when you felt like God has shown favoritism to others in your life?

Chapter 3 – Beautiful Scars

Scars are the misfortunes and mistakes of yesterday still appearing today. They are merely portraits of past calamities and memories resting on the surface. Each one is different in its own way and narrates its own story, yet, all represent past hurts. Some people are proud of their scars and wear them proudly, while some are ashamed and desperately keep them hidden from the world. Now, I can't tell you which of the two are right or wrong, but I will say that no matter if your scars represent a heroic moment or horrific moment, you should never allow your past to define your future.

While that may sound a bit cliché, it doesn't take away from the fact that it's true. In fact, not all scars are the result of being cut on the outside. A great deal of them originate from the inside out. Some people cover their scars with makeshift bandages such as alcohol, work, porn, and even religion. Society teaches us that scars are ugly, but one of my goals, and the main purpose of this book, is to teach both scarred and unscarred people how to find the beauty beneath the scars. After discussing this with a friend of mine, he wrote a poem entitled, "Beautiful Scars." The wording of his poem took my breath away as it gracefully captures my life's story and vividly displays it as a beautiful masterpiece.

"Beautiful Scars"
Beautiful is my future, but ugly was my past.
Beautiful is the sun, the rain it didn't last.
Beautiful was my recovery, addiction was my pain.
Beautiful is my Savior who removed the crimson stain.
Beautiful is my freedom, depressing were those chains.
Beautiful are my scars... Beautiful is my name.

By: Jai L.

For some reason, that poem has stuck with me since reading it. I guess it's because it helps me to see the beauty in my scars. However, some scars are more visible than others, but the memories associated with them are just as deep. This subject of scars is so massive, I decided to break it up into sections using subtitles that are associated with scars. The purpose of this is to allow my readers to analyze and understand the cycle, purpose, and origin of scars.

THE BANDAGE

One summer morning, I went on a short walk and the sun was shining brightly. The mid-summer heat torched my skin and I became thirsty. I drank the bottled water I brought with me and started to gaze at the label.

I never did this before, especially for bottled water. I was fascinated by the amount of info it gave. The label told the whole story of that bottled water: where it's from, how much was inside the bottle, what's in it, and where it was going.

I then looked at the price tag, which said 99 cents; it made me think on how society places labels and values on things. It also made me think on how I felt when labels and price tags were placed on me when I was younger. I spent most of my days in elementary trying my best to be a "good girl," most of my days in junior high trying to find myself, and a great deal of my high school days as a class clown. After trying to be a party girl in high school and the cool kid during my junior year, the name "Class Clown"'still stuck with me.

It's a title/label that I took on when I was younger, on the day my dad took me roller skating for the first time. Obviously, I couldn't skate, and I was so afraid of falling down. I will never forget reading a sign that was posted which said "Skate at your own risk!" This frightened me and I figured many people must have gotten hurt while attempting to skate. That must be why the sign was posted in plain sight. I decided that I didn't want to be their next victim, but my dad was a little upset that I wasn't skating and asked what was wrong: I simply told him my concerns, and I never will forget how Dad and his friends thought it was so funny and how they burst into laughter.

That was the first time I made adults laugh, and not only did it get me out of trouble, but it also felt good. From that point on, I started using this new found skill to cover the areas I lacked or fell short in. If my dad had known that this was what I was going to use my sense of humor for, he would never have encouraged it. The abuse I suffered as a child left me feeling ugly inside due to the inner scars. So like a bandage, I covered that area with laughter and clowning. My humor got me accepted and people wanted me around because I would make them laugh. But the truth is, it wasn't all a joking matter because while I was making people laugh, I was really keeping them away from seeing the hurt I carried deep down inside. There's an old song called, "Tears of a Clown" and that song describes my character at the time in full detail. Now, I wasn't born when Smokey Robinson wrote the lyrics, but boy did I connect with it as a child when I first heard it.

Proverbs 4:23 More than anything you guard, protect your mind, for life flows from it.

While clowning around may have helped me become accepted and fit in socially, it did nothing for me in terms of education. I had always dreamed of finishing high school and attending the one and only NYU. However, while my goals were in the right place, my grades weren't. I had to settle for the college of my community rather than the college of my choice. It pays to pay attention in school, but it's hard to pay attention while being an unpaid clown. The years of joking and trying to win people over with humor had finally caught up with me. I was a high school senior with no clue as to what to do next.

Previously, I had skated my way through difficult situations I'd faced in high school because I was one of the best basketball players in my school. Those days were quickly coming to an end because I had invested everything into procrastination and invested nothing into my education. Finally, I was confronted with the truth when I realized that the teachers who allowed me to slide were no longer able to help me. I was told that I had to do this and that or I would not graduate.

Life alone will teach us to guard our heart, yet so often we leave our mind unguarded. The enemy knows this and will use it against you. Your mind can be dangerous to your enemies when it's in action, but an idle mind is the devil's playground. I remember singing a certain song in church that says "I woke up this morning with my mind stayed on Jesus." I didn't fully understand it at the time, but now I see that my mind was so caught up with thinking about my past and my present that I couldn't focus on my future. I didn't properly prepare for my future.

This placed my dreams of attending NYU so far out of reach that it seemed hopeless. My low self-esteem didn't help the situation either, as I felt I was not smart enough to attend NYU anyway. This is the true damage of not feeling valued; sooner or later you start to believe the price tag others have placed on you. I don't know who is reading this, but whatever you do, never make the mistake of believing a lie. My grades may not have been great, but it did not reflect my true potential! I knew that I could still be great and do great things if I was willing to persevere, and that's exactly what I did. I was determined to make it to college, and nothing was going to stop me. Or so I thought.

SELF-CUTS

In spite of my circumstances, I pushed myself to do what was necessary to graduate high school. I finished strong and I did make it to college as I proclaimed I would. I was so proud of myself. However, it still wasn't enough to get me into NYU. The feeling of accomplishment was bittersweet, but it felt good to finish. My first day at Cuyahoga Community College, locally known as Tri-C, was everything I thought it would be and more. I was excited, nervous, and felt as if I could accomplish anything! The first day was a success, filled with meeting new people and basically learning the campus's layout.

It was all good, until about midweek, when I realized that none of the teachers had called my parents or questioned me about homework. That's when I figured out that this was nothing like high school because there was no one to monitor what I was doing! Most people would have jumped for joy, but I started to sink fast. Like the baby elephant I spoke of in Chapter 1, my mind had created limits and minimized my strengths and potential.

I came to believe that I had only made it this far because there was always someone there to make sure I was doing what I was supposed to do. Without that daily guidance, I was lost and thought I would surely fail. By then, I wasn't sure whether I had grown out of the class clown role or if I simply learned my lesson, but I quickly adapted to my new situation. With that, I adopted a new role by becoming a "Great Pretender." What I mean by that is, I showed up every day, but I wasn't doing what I was supposed to do. I went to school and fixed my salad in the cafeteria, then I would leave to go to a certain place to hang out for the rest of the day.

This place was called "Under the Ramp." The students called it that because it was basically a spot under a handicap ramp. It was a quiet spot where I could go and be left alone. I may have gone into college courageous and confident, but I cowered under the ramp, unconsciously wrapped in the label I had fought so hard to get rid of-- "Nothing." This time, I was not only wearing the label, I was living it. This label had returned with a vengeance, and it became the new blockade in my life because it blocked all knowledge from coming in and all of potential from getting out.

John 5:8 Jesus said to him, "Get up! Pick up your mat and walk."

This is one of my favorite Bible stories. This man had been sick for 38 years, which was 38 years of heartache, 38 years of pain, 38 years of watching others get blessed! I like the fact that it doesn't say if he was rich or poor, fat or thin, smart or uneducated, it simply states his need. To add insult to injury, the word says he sat on a porch that was designed for the sick and handicap. Like me, he sat at the ramp doing nothing. His solution to his problem was to simply sit near his miracle and complain that no one would help him reach his goal.

This is called self-cutting. It's the act of cutting yourself and complaining that no one would give you a bandage. It's the act of blaming others for your shortcomings. I was no different as I chose to sit under that ramp and watch others receive the blessings that were laid up for me. While it may not have taken me 38 years, I've learned that purpose isn't something you wait for; you must walk into it!

STITCHES

Some cuts are so severe and so deep that placing a bandage on it alone isn't enough. Some cuts have to be sewn and mended back together. Stitches are a form of help that attaches to the hurt to bring forth healing. Stitches can be aggravating and annoying because it may cause the hurt area discomfort and our initial thought is to cut the stitches. But, if we are patient and are willing to go through that discomfort, we can be healed.

My life is a testament to this because, after leaving Tri-C and doing the things I shouldn't have been doing, I ended up getting cut in bad relationships, street life, and bad decisions. Scars had become a part of my life, and like stitches, I desperately pulled myself together, waiting to be healed. I knew I had to turn my life around but wasn't sure how to do it. By now I had two daughters, a criminal record, and the odds were stacked against me. However, I was determined not to give up.

I had multiple people tell me that if I had a felony I couldn't be a truck driver, but something told me to go down and talk to them. I did just that, and I didn't cover up or hide anything because I felt what was meant to be will be. There is something about the favor of God that will open doors when you operate in the spirit of truth. I explained my situation and they told me what I needed to do, which included getting my Commercial Driver's License temps and then coming back to enroll. Now that I think about it, God had to be in control because everything worked out. I did it, even though people thought I was wasting my time, and that it wouldn't be long before I found my way back to the streets. But I knew I couldn't focus on what they were saying. I was on a mission.

When I completed truck driving school, I felt brand new! After being stuck and imprisoned with sin, vice, and habit I felt free of it all. After being drug-free for three years, I was completely focused on getting my life back on track. I had wrestled with addiction for so long that I forgot how it felt to be free. My scars had always appeared ugly to me and others. I never knew I could one day look at them as a thing of beauty. But knowing what every scar stood for and understanding the meaning behind the abuse and hardship made me see past the ugly scars and cuts. No longer did I see ugly scars, but for the first time I saw a survivor and she was beautiful.

But if you really think about it, salvation isn't found in the birth of Jesus Christ, but rather the death of him. His birth brought hope, but his death brought salvation. The events leading to his death were ugly and gruesome, leaving him bruised, scarred, and unrecognizable. The beauty in this is that I am healed because of his stripes! It is proof that good things can still come out of unfortunate situations. As I drove that truck, I realized how happy I was, but the devil is never satisfied with seeing you happy.

Yes, I was drug-free, but I was playing a deadly game because I was not connected with God. The truth of the matter was I was just happy to be clean from drugs. But my soul was in desperate need of cleansing. Sometimes, we are so deprived and absent from the good that we settle for good enough. And, at the time, being clean was good enough for me. So I had no drugs in me, but I also had no word in me. I was an empty vessel. But worse than that, my body was a clean house. Don't get me wrong, I wanted to go to church, but I wanted to do it when the time was right. However, if there was one scripture I wish I knew back then it would be:

Matthew 12:43-44 "Then it says, 'I will return to the house I left.' When it arrives, it finds the house unoccupied, swept clean and put in order. **45** Then it goes and takes with it seven other spirits more wicked than itself, and they go in and live there. And the final condition of that person is worse than the first. That is how it will be with this wicked generation."

I actually believed that I had to get good to get God, but I would soon learn that I had it all wrong, because I had to get God to get good.

"Scars are the misfortunes and mistakes of yesterday appearing today. They are merely portraits of past clamities and memories resting on the surface."

19 Do not take revenge, my dear friends, but leave room for God's wrath, for it is written: "It is mine to avenge; I will repay," says the Lord.

Do you see your scars, past hurts or present hurts as beautiful? Why?

1.) What scars do you have today that you are most proud of? Least proud of?

2.) Can you recognize the beauty your scars represent?

3.) How do you react when others show you their scars? Are you able to offer no judgment or is it difficult to look the other way regarding some of the things they have been through?

4.) What did it take for you realize that a self-cut needed stitches and not just a bandage? How did you seek the help you needed to make the repairs?

5.) Have you ever felt the need to prove to others that you were doing well, even though you were still self-medicating and not healing yourself?

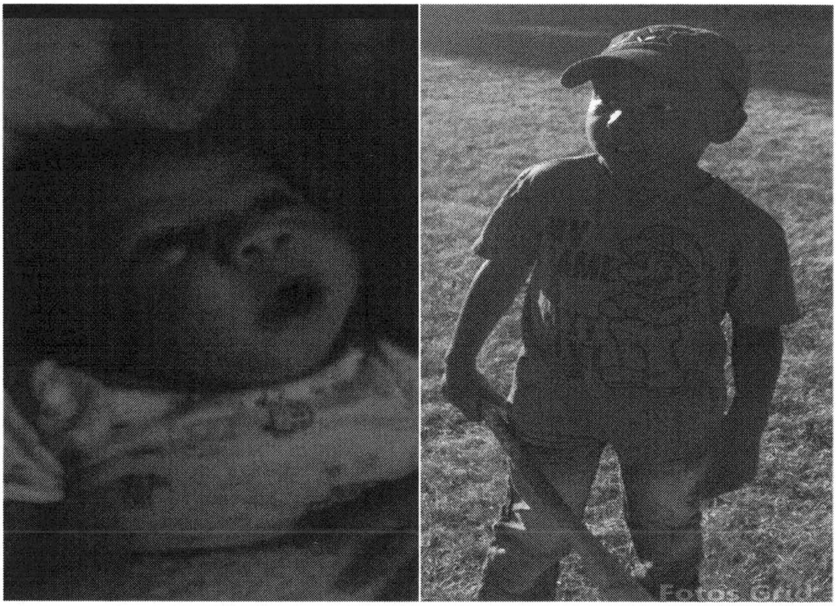

My Grandson Kameren

My Daughter Clairissa at age
3 and age 17

My Daughter Ryan at age 7
and age 24

Ryan's graduation day!!!

Mom and Dad Wedding Day
1967

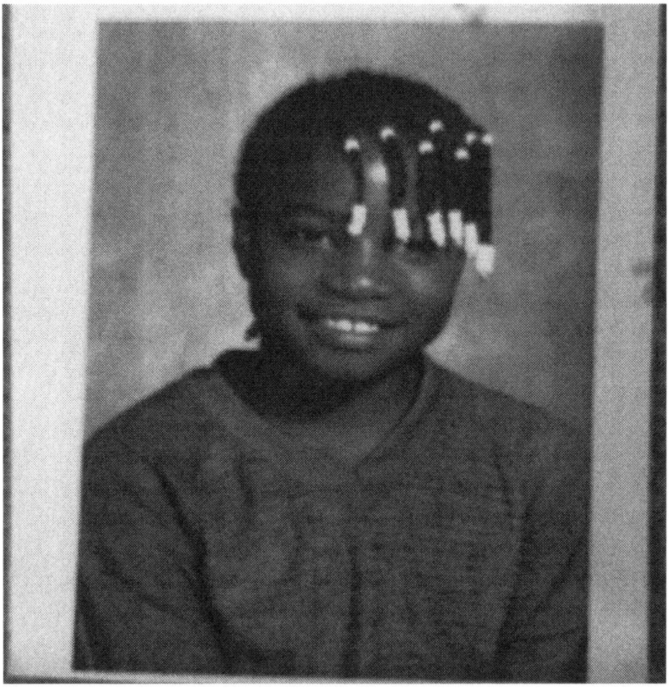

Me 1979

Me, Dad and my big brother
Bronic Jr.

Kim, Ryan and Clairissa,
1999

Me & Dad, 2016

Mom

Ryan & Julian on their
wedding day

Kim & Deb

Me and my spiritual mom
Dr. Victoria Dorsey

Min. Kim &
Deaconess Debbie

Me & My Grandson Kamren

Chapter 4 – Relapse

There's two wars within my chest
One of the spirit, one of the flesh.
One I love, one I hate.
But the one I feed, will dominate.
-Unknown author-

If there was ever a poem I could relate to, it would definitely be this one. Sadly, I know all too well about spiritual warfare. From a young age, my body has been a war zone, fighting off invaders and iniquity. Years have passed since those encounters, and I found different outlets to help me overcome my past, but they were temporary solutions. There's an old church song that says, "You can't beat God's giving, no matter how you try." It simply means that God is the giver of all things including: wealth, victories, and peace of mind. I was foolish enough to believe that a career change, AA meetings, and serenity prayers would be enough to completely free me from the devil's clutches. Friends, listen to me when I tell you this: you can change your ways, move to a new country, learn the language of that country, and even become a citizen of that country. But, if you do it without God, you haven't really moved, you've just relocated. As much as the two sound the same, they are different.

Relocate: means move to a new place and establish one's home or business there.

Move: means to go in a specified direction or manner; change position; Go; Progress; Advance.

Cancers can relocate, but the spirit of God moves. So as much as God appreciates our citizenship, he wants a relationship. Not a partnership, but a relationship! A relationship with God is what I was lacking. In today's society, we believe that time heals and forgives things, but that's not always true. When you are dealing with addiction(s), you need power, not hours. I didn't know it at the time, but powerful is our God, and without Him, you are powerless.

The Merriam-Webster dictionary defines relapse as

1: the return of an illness after a period of improvement

2: a return to bad behavior that you had stopped doing

The word relapse is widely misunderstood and misinterpreted throughout the United States. That may be closely related to the fact that most people link the word to other derogatory terms like crack head. To understand the definition of crack head, you must first understand the definition of crack. We know cocaine to be a white, powdery substance; however, crack cocaine is the crystal form of cocaine varying in color from yellow to pale rose or even white. According to an article in Addictions and Recovery.org (http://www.addictionsandrecovery.org/cocaine.htm), Dr. Steven M. Melemis, who is an addiction medicine specialist said, "Cocaine is so addictive that if you give a mouse a hit of cocaine every time it presses a lever, it will do nothing else but press that lever."

Dr. Melemis goes on to say that the mouse "won't stop for a minute to take a sip of water or a bite to eat, and eventually it will die from a cocaine overdose. The only thing that prevents people from overdosing on crack is their bank account. Once people are addicted to crack, they will sell their soul for another hit."

"It is for freedom that Christ has set us free. Stand firm, then, and do not let yourselves be burdened again by a yoke of slavery."

After years of drug bondage, I was finally free. On top of that, I was making money, lots of money, and my financial status took on a remarkable change. No longer was I scraping the bottom of the barrel trying to make ends meet. As a matter of fact, I remember my car breaking down, and I was scratching my head wondering what I was going to do. I thought to myself, "I wish I had a new car." Then it dawned on me that I had money now and could easily purchase a new car if I wanted to.

It was the first time that I realized that I was free from the old drug life. That old life offered me nothing worth having. I was consumed by the spirit of poverty because every penny I would get would go to the thing I thought I had to have: drugs. But now, things were different. I was clean, and finally I was thinking straight, at least in terms of being drug-free. I purchased that new car, and it felt good to do so. But while one desire was diminishing, another was quickly forming.

At work, I kept to myself. For the most part, people knew very little about me. They knew that I was a Christian, a single mom, and a good person, but nothing more. I remember listening to some of my coworkers during work or lunch. They would talk about going to bars or preparing for a big weekend. The thought of it would remind me of the life I was once a part of. I tried to be careful to avoid those conversations because I could see that there were some who were functioning addicts.

A functioning addict can be defined as someone who is able to hide the excesses of their alcohol or drug use. An example of this would be the functioning alcoholic who may have a good job, a secure home life, and be respected in the community, despite drinking an excessive amount of alcohol on most days. Functioning alcoholics are more common than functioning drug users and are generally able to continue this behavior longer than functioning drug users.

Honestly, I never understood the purpose of the functioning addict lifestyle. It seemed like too much work. Whenever I was out there, I was 100% committed to drug use. I'm not bragging about it, but I'm being honest. The truth is, I didn't want to risk putting that part of me out there in the face of my employers. Not to mention that I just couldn't do it. It would have been extremely hard for me to be an addict and a reliable and responsible employee. I've never been able to go out and do drugs and then report to work. Once I was out there, I was in that world. But eventually, even the ones who were trying to be functional addicts would get caught and lose their jobs. This should have been a lesson for me, but the truth is, this would not be the last relapse. It was the beginning of a 12-year downward journey that took me far from my purpose and far from God's presence.

"You took away so much and I can never get it back./That's why I made a vow that I'd never take you back./Yeah I was doing good but I was hurting people./I thought you were so pure but you were pure evil."

These are the lyrics of popular gospel rapper, Thi'sl, from his song "I Hate You." In the song, Thi'sl talks about how selling crack changed his life for the worse and how it enslaved family members, as well as himself. He also talks about how money brought pain. And now my story narrows down to how something that appeared to be so right could be so wrong. Thi'sl called drugs "pure evil," and the Bible clearly says, "For the love of money is a root of all kinds of evil. Some people, eager for money, have wandered from the faith and pierced themselves with many griefs."

1 Timothy 6:10

As I mentioned, I had a new desire; it wasn't drugs, but it was just as deceptive. Money was my new desire. Money was my new lifestyle, and worst of all, money was my new god. I figured as long as I had money, I didn't need anyone or anything. The money itself wasn't evil, and I'm not speaking against making money. In fact, money saves lives on a daily basis. However, there is a thin line between the need for money and the love of money, and I was madly in love with money. Because of this love for money, I worked as much as I could to maintain my relationship with my green lover. My father picked up on what was going on and advised me not to pick up more hours as it would keep me busy and away from God. I wish I had listened. I didn't know it, but my dad was giving me a true revelation from God. Let me reiterate what I said earlier by giving you the scripture again.

"It is for freedom that Christ has set us free. Stand firm, then, and do not let yourselves be burdened again by a yoke of slavery."

My dad was concerned about me being too busy. After doing some research, I've come to figure out what BUSY means.

Being
Under
Satan's
Yoke

The day I relapsed, it wasn't something I'd planned for. When the temptation came upon me, I was not ready at all to battle it, mainly because I had no word of God to fight it off. I was defenseless. I thought that I could "just take one" and all would be okay. I thought that I could jump head-first into the pit I once was in and come out unscathed. The Bible asks a thought provoking question:

"Can a man scoop fire into his lap and his clothes not get burned?" Proverbs 6:27

I knew the answer, but it didn't stop me from playing with fire. Even after all this time and after all of the work I'd put in. I found myself once again entangled in the yoke of bondage. And like the mouse, I was hitting that lever, again and again, all because I had developed a relationship with the creation (Money) and not with the creator (God). This time, it was worse than the other times because the enemy dispatched more demonic spirits to tarnish and violate this once clean vessel. These were the times that I stayed away from family and friends because of shame. But that drug had my priorities all mixed up because I couldn't stay away from it. Dr. Melemis said, "Once people are addicted to crack, they will sell their soul for another hit." Well, I didn't sell my soul, but the love of money placed me at risk to lose it.

"What good is it for someone to gain the whole world, yet forfeit (lose) their soul?" Matt. 16:26

At the time, I could not answer that question because I was too focused on having a certain status in society. I wanted people to see something other than my past. I wanted people to say, "Look at Kim! She is doing so well!" My life was better, but from the outside only. On the inside, two wars were developing, and the home team was losing.

It's funny how some of the things we say we would never do sometimes end up being the things we do frequently. After my last run in with drugs, I had told myself that I would never be in this predicament again! Nevertheless, there I was, repeating history. This may sound like a sad story, but let me tell you about the favor of God. Some people will experience God's favor even when they are doing wrong. People would tell me they were amazed at how far I could fall but always bounce back so quickly. I would rent or sell my car just to get money to support my addiction, but when I would call it quits, I would get an even better car. This was nothing but God showing me that if I was to simply seek Him first, all of this stuff would be added, but it took me a while to see it.

By 2004, I had relapsed more times than I could remember since 1992, and I was desperate for change. Gospel recording artist Hezekiah Walker wrote a song entitled, "Try Christ." He said, "After trying everything else and everything else failed, try Christ." After years of back and forth between step programs and being in and out of treatment centers, I just got tired. Tired of reintroducing myself, tired of explaining my story, tired of failing to succeed. I realized there was only one treatment that could help me, and it was the power of the Holy Spirit!

There's two wars within my chest
One of the spirit, one of the flesh.One I love, one I hate.
But the one I feed, will dominate.
-Unknown author-

Proverbs 6:27 CEB "Can a man scoop fire into his lap and his clothes not get burned?"

Have you ever vowed to stop an addiction or habit? What was it? Were you successful or regretful?

1.) Have you ever tried to make moves in your life without God and realized it was not in fulfillment of His will?

2.) Have you ever developed a new desire after being released from an affliction?

3.) Did it seem positive at the time until you realized you were just averting your energy to a temporary solution?

4.) Have you ever been BUSY (Being Under Satan's Yoke)? How did you free yourself?

Chapter 5 - No Holds Barred

The Lord is far from the wicked, but he hears the prayers of the righteous.
Proverbs 15:29 NIV

I guess God must have heard the prayers of my dad and others who had prayed for me. I was told that my dad stood up every Sunday morning. Wednesday night, Friday night, or whenever the church doors were open for service, putting in his request, asking God to keep me safe and to bring me safely back home. After going through torment, rejection, and more, I was finally delivered from the hold of addiction. But it wasn't an easy road.

If you are reading this and currently struggling with some form of addiction, you may be asking yourself, "How did she do it?" Truth is, I have no quick fix for you, but I do have an answer. It's free, but it will cost you a lot of time. There is no step program, but your spiritual steps must remain ordered in the Lord. It won't erase your past, but it will ensure your future. It is the never failing and always prevailing power of prayer! Like many other grandmothers before mine, my grandmother would always say, "Prayer changes things." We must be careful not to look at this as a simple cliché, but we should be sure to bury it deep within the hearts and minds of our children, so that one day, if they ever find themselves in danger or trouble, it may cry out to their memory banks and possibly save their lives.

I have hidden your word in my heart that I might not sin against you. Psalm 119:11 NIV

When my daughter was five, I remember being in an area where I used to do wrong, just walking and thinking. Even though I was not in the will of God, I still would talk to God and ask Him to take the thirst and addiction away from me. I knew I couldn't do it alone and I knew I couldn't help myself, so I asked God to send someone my way. Someone who wouldn't look down on me, someone who would be of help to me, someone I could look up to and rely on as a spiritual advisor and intercessor. I would pray for this, not even realizing that he had already encamped some of his praying soldiers in my life.

I recall this lady who used to sit on the porch on 114th Street. She would watch as the other drug addicts and myself would walk up and down her street, day and night, moving without actually going anywhere. She had a sweet spirit and a kind heart, and though she knew what was going on, she never passed judgment. Maybe she had a daughter, or son, or some relative who was walking up some other street, strung out. Maybe she was able to relate to my weakness. Maybe she smiled and prayed in hopes that someone would do the same for her loved one. Maybe she was just different.

One day, God led me to talk to her, and that's when I knew that she was able to spiritually see into the lives of others. Through speaking with me, she knew I came from a Christian background. She was able to pick up from our exchange of dialogue that I once walked with the Lord and just lost my way. She invited me to her church, and I had a strong desire to go. From that day on, I would always ask as I passed her house, "Would you pray for me."

Her response was always the same, in her sweet gentle voice, "I'm always praying for you."

There is something about the power of prayer! There is something about a stranger taking the time out of their day to think of you during prayer time. You may be saying to yourself that it's hard to believe that the isolated prayers of one old lady are what broke the chain of addiction for me. But she wasn't alone. There was the mechanic whose parking lot I would use as a shortcut, and sometimes I would stop in his shop just to get warm. There was definitely something different about him too, as he was very quiet and pleasant and never said or did anything negative against me because I was an addict.

Eventually, I found out why. This man was a man of God! A pastor! So from then on, just as I asked the lady on 114th street if she would pray for me, now I also began asking him, as I took the shortcut or stopped in to get warm, "Please pray for me."

He too would say, "I'm always praying for you."

I've shared with you how my dad would stand up and pray for me at church, but he wasn't alone. He would solicit the prayers of the congregation to pray for his daughter, and guess what? They were always praying for me.

In Chapter 1, I told you about the wood I had found to make a cross for the Easter program at church. Do you remember how I found it? Discarded from the new wood and placed in a junk pile. Do you remember how it had scars and imperfections that were clearly visible? Do you remember the label that was attached to it in big bold letters? TRASH. That five-letter word symbolized and summed up its value and fate. But to me, a simple carpenter from Cleveland, Ohio, I found use for the rejected wood. Using my skills and abilities alone, I helped to find a place for it in the house of God.

One day, I was singing a song, and out of nowhere I said within myself, "I've been changed." Even though I had drugs on me, I said "I've been changed." Even though I was around others with drugs, I could still feel Christ changing me. I've been double minded about many things in life, but on that day, my mind was made up; it was over. I felt God changing me. I felt restored.

No holds barred simply means, anything goes. It means to do whatever you have to do to get the victory, and that's exactly what I intended to do. I remember laying down at the shelter and confessing my sins to God. I recall God telling me I was forgiven. I couldn't fully explain it or put it into words at the time. Now that I'm older and a bit wiser, I can look back and see how my story of restoration and my story of the wood relates. You see, just like that beautiful wood, I was at the bottom of a junk pile, void of my value, prohibited of my purpose, and stripped of my status. And like the steel coil that rested on the old wood, my sins and shame rested heavy on me. But God saw the beauty in my blemishes, and when years of sexual abuse tried to reduce me, God rebuilt me. When the devil tried to reinjure me, God repaired me. And when everyone yelled out, "Replace her," God restored me. And behold, all things are made new.

"I knew I couldn't do it alone and I knew I couldn't help myself, so I asked God to send someone my way. Someone who wouldn't look down on me, someone who would be of help to me, someone I could look up to and rely on as a spiritual advisor and intercessor."

Mat. 9:22 Jesus turned and saw her her. "Take heart, daughter," he said. "your faith has healed you." And the woman was healed at that moment.

Have you ever been restored or had to restore someone else? Which was easier?

1.) Have you ever felt too deep in your own storm to pray for yourself? Explain.

2.) Have you ever had a moment when you could say to yourself, "I have changed?"

3.) Have you ever been able to see the beauty and potential in something others have marked as unvaluable?

Chapter 6 - Preachers, Teachers & Reachers

Matthew. 14:29 ... Then Peter got down out of the boat, walked on the water and came toward Jesus. 30 But when he saw the wind, he was afraid and, beginning to sink, cried out, "Lord, save me!" 31 Immediately Jesus reached out his hand and caught him...

I've always liked this scripture. Not so much because Peter walked on water, but it has a much deeper meaning to it. You see, at the cross, Jesus symbolically reached out to us when we were sinking in sin. This story gives an account where Jesus literally reached out to his disciple when he was sinking in doubt. Before I move on and reveal the importance of this, I want to point out something. Twelve disciples safely got on the boat and one decided to do a great work, but somewhere along the line, he got himself in some trouble. He could have cried out to the 11 that were in the safe place on the boat to pull him out of his trouble, but instead he cried out to the Lord and said, "Lord, save me!" So why is this so important? Well, it's important to know that while we may sometimes need refuge and safe dwellings, God doesn't need a safe place because he *is* the safe place. The Bible says that "The name of the Lord is a strong tower: the righteous run in and they are safe." Proverbs18:10

In a perfect world, this would be a great story. But, as many times as I've heard people preach it, it's rare to see someone live it. The reality is: even after getting cleaned up and even after confessing your sins to God, there will still be some who refuse to welcome you back in. The Bible gives us multiple stories of individuals who went astray and somehow found their way back home. Nevertheless, restoration doesn't always lead to celebration. Even after the father forgave the prodigal son, he was still met with opposition from his own brother. Even when Paul was forgiven and repositioned, he still had to deal with unforgiving Christians. So, the fact is: you may not find a safe place among those who claim to serve the same God as you, but fear not, you are safe in the arms of God. David said he would not fear while he walks through the valley because God is with him (Psalm 23:4). Peter cried out to Jesus to save him because he knew he was with him (Matt.14:30). Even the 3 Hebrew boys were not alone in the fiery furnace because God was with them in the fire (Dan. 3:25).

All of these examples show that God is with you through the good and the bad. The Bible says He is a present help in the time of trouble (Psalm 46:1). So there I was, "The Prodigal Daughter" returning home, and there was my daddy with his arms outstretched. I'll never forget how my dad held me so tight and wept. He later told me that God told him if he would just take his hands off of it, He (God) would handle it. After years of being lost and years of being in sin, God did more than just handle it, He fixed it!

I was so excited to begin my new life in Christ and I came through the door very transparent. I didn't want to hide anything! I shared a lot of information and talked about things most people would have kept secret. I figured I was in a safe place, among people who loved and accepted me, because that is what Jesus did. However, I could have never been so wrong. See, I didn't know that there were people in the church who would hold my past against me. I didn't know that, behind closed doors, they would cut me up into little pieces, yet smile to my face on Sunday mornings. I didn't know that when God began to elevate me, some would be unaccepting of it. How and why would God use me? I couldn't understand why people would laugh, doubt, and discredit me.

How is it that the world accepted me in my dirty state, yet some in the church rejected me in my clean state? If you have ever wondered this, you must first understand unhappiness. People who are unhappy with their life will find it extremely difficult to be happy about yours. To be honest, some people will hate your happiness, some people will be jealous of your joy, some people will even reject your recovery!

However, hate, jealousy, and rejection aren't the frightening part. The frightening part is that I found some of these people and attributes in church. Now, if you think the same way I used to think, you will find my last sentence shocking. It's shocking, because from our youth, we are taught that the church is supposed to love and show compassion, even when everyone else doesn't. The church is supposed to be this perfect establishment, void of any and all wrongdoing. The church helps to bring hope to the hopeless and encouragement to those who are discouraged. The church never fails. This is what I thought before my eyes were opened to a truth I had not realized. That truth is that the church is made up of imperfect people and sometimes that imperfection manifests or reveals itself in hurtful words.

I've learned, in spite of what I thought, the church can, in fact, fail. This is why it's so important to not base your happiness on the acceptance or approval of any person or organization, whether it be church, step programs, or any other entity established to help others. It also taught me that while man can fail me, God's will and word has never failed me and will not fail me.

This is made apparent in the story of The Prodigal Son. The father's love was everlasting and he welcomed the son back home. However, the brother wasn't as forgiving or as merciful. It's usually those close to you who will do you the most harm. In this walk, you may encounter people like that, but be steadfast and unmovable and continue to abide in the work of the

Lord, knowing your labor isn't in vain. This is what I had to do concerning those who rejected me. For those of you who are currently in this situation, I will be honest and say it's not easy, but it doesn't have to be hard either. Be sure to make a note of what I'm going to say next... When dealing with a restored and renewed soul, celebration is necessary! There is no way around it, if you are a child of God who has been delivered from sin, vice, and habit, celebration is necessary! The word tells us to weep with those who weep and rejoice with those who rejoice! The father of the prodigal son said it best when he was speaking to the unforgiving son. He simply said, "But we had to celebrate and be glad, because this brother of yours was dead and is alive again; he was lost and is found.' " Luke 15:32 NIV

What the father said was so profound and it carried a lot of weight. The prodigal son had been away for quite some time. It's possible that people may have assumed that he was dead. I was no different because I stayed away so long that people thought I had fallen off the face of this Earth. Just like the song, my life could have been a sad story with a tragic end but God wouldn't allow it to be. It took the prodigal son until he remembered his father's house to turn his life around. I remembered my grandmother's stories about the great loving and forgiving man named Jesus. I remembered how much he loves me. I remembered how much I wanted to be his friend and that's what I held on to. I knew that the Bible says that if I am a friend of the world, I couldn't be a friend of God. I had to let it go and I couldn't allow the immaturity and lack of love from others to stop me from reaching my goal.

This is what I want to leave with you in this chapter: Never give up on yourself, even if everyone else gives up on you, *never* give up on yourself. As long as there is a God Who sits high and looks down low, there is no pit that is so deep that He can't reach down and pull you out. "I put all my hope in the Lord. He leaned down to me; He listened to my cry for help. He lifted me out of the pit of death, out of the mud and filth, and set my feet on solid rock. He steadied my legs. He put a new song in my mouth, a song of praise for our God. Many people will learn of this and be amazed; they will trust the Lord. Those who put their trust in the Lord, who pay no attention to the proud or to those who follow lies, are truly happy!" Psalms 40:1-4 CEB

"So there I was, "The Prodigal Daughter" returning home, and there was my daddy with his arms outstretched."

For whosoever shall call upon the name of the Lord shall be saved. Romans 10:13 KJV

Has anyone ever reached out to you?
What was the result?

1.) Have you ever experienced a time when even after apologizing to someone, they still refused accept your apology? What lesson did you learn about forgiveness from this? Did that teach you to be more forgiving to others?

2.) Have you ever had an experience with an unforgiving Christian? What did that teach you about the imperfections in God's house?

3.) Think of a time when God was with you through the good and the bad. Were you aware of His presence while you were going through?

4.) Now think of a Prodigal Son/Daughter experience you've had or been a part of. How grateful were you to be welcomed back with no judgment? How good did it feel to be the one who forgave with no judgment?

5.) Have you ever experienced a time when someone close to you (like a brother) was not forgiving of you when you expected them to be? What did that teach you about human imperfection and the importance of forgiveness?

Chapter 7- Necessary

The word "necessary" means to require to be done, achieved, or present. It shows the importance of something by expressing the essential, mandatory, and imperative need of something or someone. As we learned in Chapter 6, the father of the prodigal son said to his other son, "It was necessary for us to rejoice." Why was it necessary? Because it was a matter of life and death. He said, "Your brother who we thought was dead is now alive! The same brother who we thought was lost, is now found! Therefore as the father and ruler of this house, I proclaim that it is imperative, mandatory and of a necessity that the entire house rejoices and proclaims the mighty works of God!"

When I was out in the world, the devil tried to get me to believe that drugs were necessary in my life, when the truth was: I didn't need drugs - drugs needed me! Without my participation, there is no high. Without my willingness to engage in such acts, there is no addiction. This is why I say that drugs needed me, because I was the vessel being used by this parasitic intruder. But, while things looked hopeless, God had a plan. I personally couldn't see the outcome or purpose of His plan, but it was necessary for me to go through it in order for me to get through it. All the while, I did not know that one day my story would be read by others who, out of necessity, are going through or have gone through, some type of adversity.

I am reminded of the necessity of adversity when I hear the singer Fantasia sing gospel music. She sings with so much passion, conviction, and truth that tugs at the heartstrings and emotions of the audience. I am encouraged by her lyrics because I know that it's not just some fabricated story, but it's her testimony and it just sends chills down my spine. She sings a song titled "Necessary" which speaks about every positive and negative thing that we may have encountered, and still have yet to encounter, on this journey called life. Too often, testimonies are partially conveyed, delivering only part of the story. Some believe they can't share their testimony if it doesn't end with "but God." Don't you know that God's timing isn't our timing? And that the trying of your faith builds patience? So even if you are still in the storm, you are still able to encourage another who may also be in the storm. However, there are some who take off running as soon as they see a gray cloud. I don't know why some people feel that the only way to survive a storm is to outrun one! The truth is, even if you stand still and do nothing, the storm will eventually pass over you because trouble doesn't last always. However, we are taught to run at the sight of adversity, not knowing that having a vast knowledge of danger is better than having an awareness or fear of it. What do you mean minister? Well, if I'm aware of danger or if I fear danger, I may be able to avoid it IF I see it coming. But the devil always tries to catch us when we're not looking and this is where knowledge and understanding becomes a valuable tool. You see, if I have a detailed understanding of the storm, I can not only help myself, but I can also help others, while near or even in the storm myself.

There are a handful of intelligent, knowledgeable, and helpful meteorologists who are misunderstood because of their dangerous job as "Storm Chasers." While the storm runners are running from the storm, these courageous individuals are chasing the storm. Not because they are solely thrill seekers or crazy, but because they know that the key to surviving the storm is within it. They will tell you that while they fear and respect the sheer power of the storm, they fight that fear with facts. They may not be able to tell you the exact time and day the storm will appear, but once it does appear, they can make a knowledgeable and informative prediction as to where it's going. I don't know about you, but I thank God for the storm chaser today, because their courage keeps us safe and their research keeps us informed! Like many of you, I was a storm runner. I tried to avoid and outrun the storm as much as I could. Sometimes I escaped, but most of the time I was caught in its whirlwind, tossed back and forth in what seemed like a never-ending cycle. It was like the popular movie, The Wizard of Oz, and I was

Dorothy, desperately trying to make it home.

That storm took me so far away from home and family, but one day I stopped running and decided to become a storm chaser. I had to gain knowledge of the storm. While on the road to freedom and restoration, I came across a man who is the storm stopper. He showed me my calling and destiny and removed the crimson stain within my heart and the taste of sin within my soul. He told me that in order to kill the storm in my life, I must first deal with the storm in my life. Dealing with it was the hardest thing, because it took me back to where it all started. Let me tell you this as the spirit is speaking to me. You can't finish anything you haven't started! I realized that even though I had forgiven my attacker, I still had to forgive myself! I had to realize that I was not guilty! And then I just started working my way down my timeline until I got to the finish line. I found myself back with family and realized that there is no place like home!

So know that you are still usable in the kingdom of God, as the only difference between a stumbling block and a stepping stone is how you use it. Your storm can be used to evoke fear into the lives of others or be used as a teachable tool needed to place us in a position to put our total dependence on God. This isn't always easy because we, as humans, try to fix things for ourselves, only to call on God when we realize we only made things worse. But when we realize the true meaning of this word as necessary, we can understand the importance of putting God first in everything we do. The Bible says to acknowledge God in everything we do and not to lean (trust) on our own understanding. In other words, it is necessary to seek God's counsel, approval, and wisdom when dealing with the storms of life. If your testimony is without a test, you may be running in the wrong direction!

We all will face some types of storms in our lifetime and, with the help of God, you too can make it through. The question is, after making it through the storm, how do we stay on course and what preventive measures can be taken to avoid future storms? The truth is: we can't prevent storms from coming. Jesus tells us, "I've said these things to you so that you will have peace in me. In the world you have distress. But be encouraged! I have conquered the world." John 16:33

However, while we may not be able to prevent the storm, we are able to better prepare ourselves by surrounding ourselves with people who we can be held accountable to. Through the years, I have had an amazingly wonderful God-given support team that consisted of my children: Ryan and Clairissa, my Dad, and my best friend Deb, who just would not give up on me. Although there was a time when Dad and Deb proved to be my biggest enablers, now that I look back, they were just in a position of looking at a young woman who they wanted so badly to save. But God had to teach them something about trying to save someone in their own strength. The Bible tells us to "work out our own salvation" Phil 2:12. God had to show them that it was necessary for me to go through some things and that they really were interfering with His plan. God told Abraham and his wife that he was going to make him "father of many nations." This seemed impossible because Abraham and his wife were old. In fact, the thought of this seemed so crazy that Abraham's wife had a good laugh at the very thought. "So Sarah laughed to herself, thinking, I'm no longer able to have children and my husband's old."

"The LORD said to Abraham, "Why did Sarah laugh and say, 'Me give birth? At my age?' Is anything too difficult for the LORD? When I return to you about this time next year, Sarah will have a son.""

Some of you who are reading this have received a word from God, but because it sounds crazy, you just can't picture it happening. One thing you have to realize is that God talk is crazy talk! God will speak to you about millions when your bank account is in the negative! God will talk to you about nations when you don't even have one child! God will tell you to go into business, after you just bounced a check! God will talk to you about mansions after checking into a homeless shelter! God will tell you he's about to bless you with a new car when you don't even own a bike! God! God! GOD!!! There is power in his name! Demons tremble at his name!

Sometimes God will reveal his end plan to us, however, when we don't see immediate results, we feel we have to help God out. That is what Abraham and Sarah did. They tried to fix something for God, so his wife brought in her handmaiden as an alternative so that Abraham could have children through her and the prophecy would be fulfilled. Let me tell you something, God doesn't need us to cover for him. If he said it, he is faithful and just to perform it! It was God who saw me walking the streets, spiritually deprived and shackled by drug addiction, wishing I could turn back the hands of time and go to a place where I had never touched a drug or drink and never experienced being sexually abused. It's sad to say that that would have placed me at around the age of two. My dark journey began around the age of three when the babysitter robbed me of my innocence. God heard their prayers just as He had heard the prayers of the lady on 114th Street and the pastor who owned the mechanic shop. While they were praying, I was asking Him to help me and He did! He didn't have to go around what he said, he didn't have to use anyone else because my blessing came through me! I don't know where you are right now, but if God told you he would bless you, lay hands on yourself right now and say, "It will come through me!" Not through my mama, not through my daddy, but through me! Why? Because God said so!

If you're reading this book and have a loved one who is struggling with issues, please remember that God doesn't need for you to get in His way. Just continue to pray for them as my loved ones finally learned to pray for me. There is purpose in God's plan. Jesus came for people like us. Mark 2:17 says, "When Jesus heard this, He told them, 'Healthy people don't need a doctor- sick people do. I have come not to call those who think they are righteous, but those who know they are sinners.'"

To show how God works...My best friend Deb had never had a relationship with our Lord and Savior Jesus Christ. Her seeing my life go downhill right before her eyes was enough to send her to her knees. It was necessary for these traumatic events to unfold right before her eyes. She has always been a kind person with a beautiful spirit and I'm so glad she's been a faithful friend to me and my family. Today, she's a powerful missionary and I often like to tease her by saying that I was her first missionary case. God uses Deb in such a mighty way. She demonstrates faithfulness. I'm sure many would have lost their best friend, but I'm blessed to say I still have mine. Many have lost their children, but I'm blessed to say I still have mine. Many have lost their minds, but I still have mine.

Now, I need to finish off by telling you about my two amazing daughters, Ryan and Clairissa. These young ladies had to experience part of their lives with a mother who would disappear for long periods of time. There are more things than I would like to think of that I missed. Yes, it hurts to even think about it and guess what? They don't remind me of any of it. It's almost as if we never missed a beat. But the reality of this is that they really have been protecting my feelings and disregarding their own. Once The Holy Spirit showed me that, it was then when I had to sit with them and let them know that it was ok to tell me how all of this has affected them. Ryan's experience is different from

Clairissa's. For half of Ryan's life, I was bound by drug abuse. For most of Clairissa's life, she has had the drug-free, saved mom. My girls are precious to me. I admire their strength and my prayer is that God will continue to grow them in Him. We, as a family, have been on the road of healing and growth.

So for every piece of pain I ever experienced, I now know that it was necessary to mold me into the woman God has called me to be. The enemy wanted to take me out, but God extended grace and mercy towards me and turned a mess into a miracle.

"So for every piece of pain I ever experienced, I now know that it was necessary to mold me into the woman God has called me to be. The enemy wanted to take me out, but God extended GRACE and MERCY towards me and turned a mess into a miracle."

"You intended to harm me, but God intended it for good to accomplish what is now being done, the saving of many lives" (Gen. 50:20 NIV)

IT WAS NECESSARY!

Name something that happened to you that you feel was necessary for spiritual growth. How did it impact your life?

Contact Information
Rev. Kimberly A. Walker
beautifulscars2714@yahoo.com
www.beautifulscars100.com